First published by Allen & Unwin in March 2001
This edition published by Whitecap Books 2001

National Library of Canada Cataloguing in Publication Data

Van Loon, Joan.
The chocolate lovers

ISBN 1-55285-233-4

1. Cookery (Chocolate) – Juvenile literature. I. Stewart, Chantal. II. Gaté, Gabriel, 1955– III. Title.
TX767.C5V35 2001   j641.6'374   C2001–910491–X

Designed and typeset by Sandra Nobes
Printed in China by Everbest

Approximate Conversions

1 metric cup = 250 ml = 9 oz

1 cup brown sugar = 160 g = 6 oz
1 cup sugar = 220 g = 8 oz
1 cup all-purpose flour = 150 g = 5.5 oz
1 cup cocoa = 150 g = 5.5 oz
1 cup walnuts = 120 g = 4.5 oz
1 cup rice = 250 g = 9 oz
1 cup chocolate chips = 180 g = 6.5 oz

Oven Temperature

200°C = 400°F
180°C = 350°F
150°C = 300°F
100°C = 210°F

Dear Readers

Joan, Chantal and I are all chocolate lovers and we love cooking with chocolate. ❧ We recommend that you wash your hands before cooking—and remember to lick the bowl afterwards! We always do. ❧ All these delicious chocolate recipes have been tested using bittersweet chocolate, cocoa powder and other ingredients from our local supermarket. The recipes are for kids to prepare with the help of an adult, or for adults to prepare for children. But adults must ask children first before tasting the food! ❧ We hope you like Joan's story, Chantal's illustrations, and cooking the yummy dishes.

❧ Love from the three of us,
Gabriel the Chef

Gabriel's Recipes

My mom tells everyone I'm a top cook.
That's why she sent me to the Master Class for chefs.

A few of my friends were there, but there was one girl
I'd never seen before.

Her name was Marian Madeleine Monkhouse.

Hot Chocolate

¾ cup milk or soy milk • 2 tsp cocoa • 1 tsp sugar

Bring milk to a simmer. Whisk in cocoa and sugar and pour into a cup.
It is lovely in winter or when you feel cold.

SERVES 1

"*Bonjour*, everyone," said Gabriel, who was the master of the class. "This six-week course is all about the pleasures of cooking with chocolate."

We dressed ready to cook. Marian Madeleine Monkhouse looked amazing.

Chocolate Truffles

2 tbsp rich cream ♦ 1 tbsp milk
4½ oz bittersweet chocolate, chopped ♦ ½ cup cocoa

Bring cream and milk to the boil in a saucepan and on low heat stir in chocolate until it has all melted. Transfer preparation to a bowl and refrigerate for 30–40 minutes, stirring occasionally. It will stiffen like thick icing. ♥ Using a teaspoon, scoop mounds of chocolate the size of a large macadamia nut onto a tray lined with baking paper. ♥ Place cocoa in a bowl. Using a fork, lift each truffle and roll it in the cocoa. To make them round, roll the coated truffles quickly between your hands. Don't press too hard. Then roll truffles again in the cocoa and refrigerate until required.

MAKES ABOUT 20 TRUFFLES

"Chocolate has a thousand uses," said Gabriel. "You can...

melt it, spread it, shape it, shred it ... dust it, drizzle it, stir it, curl it grate it, paste it, fill it, bake it ... chip it, shake it, beat it, break it.

Chocolate Milk Shake

1 cup homogenized milk ◆ 2 scoops vanilla ice cream
2 tsp cocoa powder or 2 tbsp grated chocolate

Place milk, ice cream and cocoa or grated chocolate in a blender or food processor and blend on high speed for 30 seconds. ♥ Pour milk shake into a tall glass and serve. It makes a cool treat on a hot summer's day.

SERVES 1

Or you can simply…

put a tiny piece in a box, wrapped in foil, tied with string…
and give it to someone you love."

At the word "love", my friends whistled and hooted. Marian Madeleine Monkhouse rolled her eyes.

Chocolate Fudge Brownies

1 tbsp melted butter to grease pan ✤ 7 oz bittersweet chocolate, broken into small pieces
⅔ cup butter, cut into small cubes ✤ 1 cup brown sugar ✤ 2 eggs ✤ 1 cup all-purpose flour, sifted
1 cup walnut halves, chopped ✤ ½ cup almonds, chopped ✤ 2 tbsp icing sugar for dusting

Butter the sides and base of a 9 x 13 inch baking pan and line the base with parchment paper. Preheat oven to 350°F. ❦ Melt chocolate and butter in a bowl resting over a saucepan of hot water, stirring until smooth. Remove from heat and beat in sugar and eggs. Stir in flour, walnuts and almonds. ❦ Pour mixture into the prepared pan and bake in preheated oven for 25 minutes. ❦ Allow to cool in the pan, then dust with icing sugar and cut into 30 rectangles. ❦ They're great for birthday parties!

MAKES 30 BROWNIES

"There is nothing so exciting as chocolate," Gabriel said.
"Some people eat it for energy…

Chocolate Rice Pudding

1 cup medium grain rice ❦ 4 cups milk ❦ 3 tbsp sugar ❦ 1 tsp grated orange zest
3½ oz bittersweet chocolate, cut into small pieces

Place rice in a large saucepan of water. Bring water to the boil and boil for 4 minutes.
Drain. ❦ Bring milk to a simmer in a large non-stick saucepan. Add rice and orange zest
and stir. Bring to a simmer, then cover pan for about 30 minutes. Be careful in the last few
minutes that the rice does not stick or burn. ❦ Stir in sugar and chocolate until melted.
Pour into a deep serving dish and serve either hot or cold. I prefer it cold.
It's lovely with vanilla ice cream or dusted with icing sugar.

SERVES 6–8

others, for courage.

Chocolate Chip Cookies

½ cup unsalted butter, softened ❦ ⅓ cup brown sugar ❦ ½ cup sugar
1 tsp finely grated orange rind or ½ tsp vanilla extract ❦ 1 large egg
1½ cups all-purpose flour, sifted ❦ 1½ tsp baking powder ❦ ½ tsp baking soda
¼ tsp salt ❦ 1 cup chocolate chips

Preheat oven to 325°F. ❦ Cream butter with both types of sugar and the orange rind or vanilla until creamy. Mix in egg thoroughly. Sift the flour with baking powder, soda and salt. Mix in flour and add chocolate chips. ❦ Place small tablespoonful of the mixture 1 inch apart on a buttered baking sheet and bake in the preheated oven for about 8–10 minutes. ❦ Remove from oven and leave to cool on the baking sheet for 2 minutes before transferring to a cake rack. Store in an airtight container.

MAKES ABOUT 20 COOKIES

"Some say it's the food of angels…

Chocolate Mousse

5½ oz bittersweet chocolate • 2 tbsp whipping cream • 3 egg yolks • 4 egg whites
a small pinch of cream of tartar • 1 tbsp sugar

Break chocolate into small pieces and place in a glass bowl with cream. Cover with plastic wrap and melt in the microwave for about 30 seconds. Stir briefly, then continue to microwave for 5–10 seconds at a time, until the chocolate is soft. 🍮 Add the yolks and combine until smooth. 🍮 Add a pinch of cream of tartar to the egg whites and beat them with the electric beater. When they are fairly firm, add sugar and continue beating until stiff peaks form. 🍮 Using a large metal spoon, gently incorporate a quarter of the egg whites into the chocolate preparation, then carefully fold in the rest of the whites. 🍮 Gently spoon the mixture into 6 small cups or into a suitable bowl and leave to set in the refrigerator for at least 2 hours.

SERVES 6

12

or of devils—"

Chocolate Sauce

½ cup water • *2 tbsp sugar* • *5 tbsp cocoa* • *3 tbsp whipping cream*

Place water, sugar and cocoa in a saucepan and bring to the boil, stirring well to mix in the cocoa. Add cream and boil for ten seconds, mixing well. Pour sauce into a bowl and cool, then refrigerate until required. 💙 If the sauce is too thick, add a little cold milk. Serve sauce with cakes, pancakes and muffins. It is nice served hot with ice cream.

SERVES ABOUT 6

"Chocolate is for lovers!" I shouted.
"Mmm...!" said Marian Madeleine Monkhouse.

Chocolate Pudding

3½ oz bittersweet chocolate, broken into small pieces • 2½ oz butter, cut into small cubes
2 large eggs • 1 egg yolk • ½ cup sugar
2 tsp finely chopped orange zest • 2 tbsp cornstarch, sifted
a little extra butter to grease 6 half-cup soufflé molds

Preheat oven to 325°F. ❧ Melt chocolate and butter in a bowl over a pan of hot water and whisk until smooth. ❧ Beat eggs, egg yolk, sugar and orange zest for about 4 minutes until light and fluffy. ❧ Gently mix melted chocolate into egg mixture, then fold in cornstarch. Spoon into buttered molds and place molds on a baking sheet. ❧ Cook in preheated oven for 20 minutes. ❧ Serve with a little cream or ice cream.

SERVES 6

14

My friends rattled their cake pans and banged their bowls.
Marian Madeleine Monkhouse closed her eyes.

Chocolate Chunk Muffins

*½ cup sugar • 1 cup milk • 2 tbsp sour cream • 2 oz butter, melted • 1 large egg
2 cups all-purpose flour • 2 tsp baking powder • ½ tsp baking soda • 2 tbsp cocoa
⅔ cup chocolate chunks • a little extra butter to grease a 12-pan muffin tin*

Preheat oven to 400°F. ♥ In a bowl mix sugar, milk, cream,
butter and egg. ♥ Sift flour, baking powder, soda and cocoa together in a large bowl.
Make a well in the centre and pour the milk mixture into the well. Mix with a wooden
spoon until just combined. It is important not to overmix. Stir in chocolate chunks, then
spoon mixture immediately into your greased muffin tin. Bake in preheated oven for about
20 minutes. ♥ Turn cooked muffins out onto a cake rack and enjoy them still warm.

MAKES 12 MUFFINS

We practiced using the utensils: spatulas,
pastry brushes, beaters, whisks and knives.
Things started to get out of control.

"Watch what you are doing, *s'il vous plaît*," said Gabriel.

Chocolate and Coconut Crackles

3½ oz margarine ◆ *2 cups Rice Krispies* ◆ *¾ cup icing sugar*
2 tbsp cocoa ◆ *½ cup desiccated coconut*

Place margarine in a medium saucepan and melt on low heat. ❦ Gently stir in Rice
Krispies, icing sugar, cocoa and coconut until well combined. ❦ Remove from heat
and spoon mixture into 12 paper muffin cups. Set in the refrigerator.

MAKES ABOUT 12

Everyone was covered in chocolate.
Except Marian Madeleine Monkhouse.

Chocolate Meringues

3 large egg whites ❧ pinch of cream of tartar ❧ ½ cup cup sugar
½ cup icing sugar, sifted with 2 tbsp cocoa powder

Preheat oven to 300°F. ❧ Line two flat baking sheets with parchment paper. ❧ Whisk egg whites and cream of tartar until the whites begin to stiffen. Gradually add half of the sugar and beat until the whites are shiny and becoming firmer, then beat in icing sugar and cocoa with remaining sugar. ❧ Place tablespoonsful of mixture on the parchment paper. Place sheet in preheated oven and cook for 20 minutes. Then reduce temperature to 200°F and cook for a further 60 minutes. ❧ Switch oven off and leave meringues to dry in the oven for 2–3 hours before storing them in an airtight container.

MAKES ABOUT 15 MERINGUES

At the end of the day, we took home what we had made.

"What happened to my cake king?" Mom cried. Dad suggested we play frisbees in the park.

Chocolate Sponge Cake

2 tbsp cream ❧ 2 oz bittersweet chocolate, chopped ❧ ⅛ tsp baking soda
2 tbsp butter, cut into small pieces ❧ 4 eggs ❧ ½ cup plus 2 tbsp sugar
⅔ cup all-purpose flour, sifted

Preheat oven to 350°F. ❧ You need a buttered and floured cake pan about 8 inches in diameter. ❧ Place cream in a saucepan and bring to the boil. Reduce heat and stir in chocolate. When chocolate has just melted, remove from heat and stir in baking soda and butter until melted. ❧ Place eggs in a large bowl. Add sugar and, using an electric beater, beat for 5–6 minutes or until the mixture drops in a thick ribbon. Gently mix in melted chocolate. ❧ Add sifted flour all at once and, using a rubber spatula, fold in gently but quickly. Don't overmix. Pour mixture into prepared pan and smooth the top. Bake in preheated oven for about 30 minutes. ❧ When the sponge is cooked, remove from oven and cool for a few minutes. Run a blade around the edge and tip gently onto a wire rack. Serve with fruit, cream or ice cream.

SERVES 6–8

Week after week, I shared a workbench with Marian Madeleine Monkhouse. Whatever I made, I made for her.

I decided I would become the chocolate cake king. She would be my queen.

Chocolate Chip Cupcakes

¾ cup butter, cut into small cubes ♣ 2 tsp finely chopped orange zest ♣ ¾ cup sugar
3 large eggs ♣ 1 cup all-purpose flour, sifted ♣ ¾ tsp baking powder ♣ ⅓ cup chocolate chips
1 cup icing sugar ♣ about 2 tbsp water ♣ 3 tbsp chocolate sprinkles
12 muffin-size, paper or foil muffin cups

Preheat oven to 350°F. ♣ Beat butter, orange zest and sugar until creamy. Beat in eggs, one at a time. Sift flour and baking powder together. Fold in flour, but don't overmix. Stir in chocolate chips. ♣ Carefully spoon mixture into 12 paper or foil muffin cups, placed on a baking sheet, and bake in preheated oven for 15–20 minutes, then allow cupcakes to cool. ♣ Mix icing sugar and water in a bowl. Spread icing over cupcakes and decorate with chocolate sprinkles.

MAKES 12 SMALL CAKES

Before the last lesson, Gabriel asked everyone to prepare
a chocolate recipe at home and bring it to class.
"*Pour le festival du chocolat*," he said.

I studied the recipe books. I made my choice.
I would create a chocolate cake sensation
and give it to Marian Madeleine Monkhouse.

As I prepared to cook, Gabriel's words ran through my head. "Always use the freshest ingredients."

Strawberries Dipped in Chocolate

10 large strawberries ❤ *3½ oz semisweet chocolate, broken into small pieces*

Wash strawberries in cold water and leave the stems on. Dry strawberries gently with paper towel. ❤ Place chocolate pieces in a bowl. Place bowl over a saucepan of simmering water and melt chocolate, whisking it well until very smooth. Remove from heat. ❤ Dip strawberries in chocolate to lightly coat two-thirds of each berry. Place strawberries on parchment paper to cool. ❤ Enjoy them with your best friends.

MAKES 10 STRAWBERRIES

But…

There were weevils in the flour, the milk had gone sour,
the hens wouldn't lay and I only had a day!

What could I do?
"A cook must be resourceful,"
Gabriel had said.
So I sat down and I thought hard.

Chocolate Yogurt

2 oz chocolate of your choice ❧ 1½ cups plain thick yogurt
2 tbsp sugar ❧ 1 tbsp milk

Grate or chop chocolate finely. ❧ Whip yogurt in a bowl with sugar and milk for
30 seconds. Stir in grated chocolate and serve.

SERVES 2

If there are weevils in the flour, if the milk's gone sour, try to get your hens to lay. Wake them early in the day.

Special Easter Egg Cake

1 chocolate sponge cake, see page 18 ❦ 2 tbsp sugar ❦ 1 cup whipped cream
1 quantity of chocolate icing, see page 26 ❦ 1 cup chocolate sprinkles
8 medium chocolate eggs ❦ 2 tbsp icing sugar for dusting

Cut sponge through horizontally in two halves. ❦ Gently whisk sugar into whipped cream. Spread cream on base of cake, then top with the other cake half. ❦ Spread chocolate icing over top and sides of the cake. Pat chocolate sprinkles around the sides of the cake. ❦ Remove wrapping from eggs. Gently push eggs slightly into the icing so that it holds the eggs. Allow the icing to set for 1 hour. Just before serving, dust cake with icing sugar.

SERVES 6–8

A cook must be creative.

Heart-shaped flourless Chocolate Cake

½ tbsp melted butter to grease pan ❀ a little flour to dust pan ❀ 1 cup ground almonds
2 tbsp whipping cream ❀ 3 oz bittersweet chocolate, broken into small pieces
2 eggs, separated ❀ ¼ cup sugar ❀ ½ cup raisins ❀ pinch of cream of tartar
icing sugar to dust cake

Preheat oven to 350°F. ❀ Grease a 7½ inch heart-shaped cake pan with melted butter.
Line the base with parchment paper and grease paper with butter. Dust the paper and
sides of the pan with flour. ❀ Put cream in a small pan and bring to the boil. Remove
from heat and stir in chocolate until it melts. ❀ (*Continued opposite*)

At last it was ready.

My heart-shaped, triple-layered, double-dipped, Chocolate Lovers' Cake, filled with cream and topped with strawberries...

for Marian Madeleine Monkhouse.

Using an electric mixer, beat egg yolks and sugar for about 4 minutes until fluffy and white. ❦ Add the chocolate mixture, ground almonds and raisins and combine gently. ❦ Beat egg whites with cream of tartar until they form stiff peaks. Fold beaten whites into the chocolate mixture, then pour into prepared cake pan. ❦ Gently flatten top and bake in preheated oven for 35 minutes. ❦ Allow the cake to cool for about 20 minutes before carefully turning it out onto a rack. ❦ Dust generously with icing sugar, ice with chocolate icing, or decorate with cream and strawberries, see page 26–27.

SERVES 6

I raced to class.
My heart was flipping.

Chocolate Icing

*½ cup whipping cream ❧ 3½ oz bittersweet chocolate, chopped
1 tsp unsalted butter*

In a saucepan bring cream to the boil. Reduce heat and mix in chocolate until it has all melted. Remove from heat and whisk in butter. Allow to cool slightly. ❧ Meanwhile, place the cake on a cake rack. Gently pour icing over cake, letting it spread by itself over and down the sides of the cake or spread it with a metal spatula.

ENOUGH FOR 1 CAKE

As I threw open the door, Gabriel was speaking.
"Presentation is *très importante*..."

Delicious Decorations

It is easier to decorate a cake when the icing is still soft and not quite set. Top icing carefully with your favorite decorations, such as sprinkles, M & Ms, Smarties or chocolate chunks. ❦ Dried or glacé fruits, like apricots, pears and cherries, add rich color to a cake, as do berries, like raspberries, blueberries, blackberries and, of course, strawberries. ❦ Other clever decorations are nuts, such as almonds, cashews, hazelnuts, macadamias and brazil nuts. Grated white or dark chocolate is also nice. Sometimes chefs even use tiny bits of real gold leaf for very special cakes. ❦ Cakes decorated with cream must be kept refrigerated until just before serving. ❦ And, most importantly, don't forget to lick the bowl before washing it!

"Oh no!" I screamed.

"Oh non!" Gabriel cried.

"Oh no!" my friends all wailed.

"Oh yes!"
said Marian Madeleine Monkhouse.

"As I was saying," Gabriel continued,
"presentation is important,
but the proof of the chocolate cake
is in the taste of it."